LEARNING TO

SOAR

CREATING STRATEGY THAT INSPIRES
INNOVATION AND ENGAGEMENT

JACQUELINE M. STAVROS
GINA HINRICHS

AUTHORS' DEDICATION
We dedicate this book to our parents,
our husbands, and our children who
provide us the courage to soar.
Jacqueline M. Stavros, DM
jstavros@comcast.net
Gina Hinrichs, Ph.D.
ghinrichs517@gmail.com

SOAR INSTITUTE

www.soar-strategy.com
Designer / Alisann Marshall
marshallartsfamily@twc.com
Illustrator / Mara Wedekind
mara@stallardstudio.com

"In today's digital world, SOAR works with global team members. The results: strategic direction and strategies for growth. This book is updated with new research and applications to easily make SOAR part of your strategic toolkit."

– Ron Reidy, Senior Advisor, Dell

"I use the SOAR framework for all my strategic planning engagements. It is a practical approach to whole system engagement. Results: high engagement, generated positive energy, strengthen relationships, and successful implementation of the plan. I was excited to discover the SOAR coaching framework. A great reminder that strategy needs to be thought of as both a daily practice and a future direction."

– Maureen McKenna, Founder, Return on Energy, Toronto, Ontario

"This book offers an intuitively useful framework that is innovative and engaging. It is an excellent tool for those facilitating and leading change. I used it with an Opioid Crises Response Workgroup to develop a response plan to the epidemic facing the United States. The SOAR approach resonated with the team and worked beautifully!"

– Steven H. Cady, Ph.D., Professor, Bowling Green State University Founder, NEXUS4change

"We continue to learn in this book why SOAR is distinguished from traditional strategic planning approaches due to its generative nature and the inclusion of stakeholders. SOAR conversations create a positive frame for individuals, organizations, and communities and produce new perspectives and creative ideas to grow individuals, teams, organizations, and industries! I have supplied the Board of Education with copies of the original *Thin Book of SOAR*. With this book, I plan to do the same for more leadership teams, boards, organizations, and communities. I am struck by the immense scope of the usefulness of SOAR to organizations of all descriptions and particularly to business, industry, and education. The arrival of this book is an event to be treasured and studied!"

– Dick Marburger, Ph.D., President Emeritus, Lawrence Technological University Past President, Engineering Society of Detroit

"Our hospital learned how to use the Quick SOAR presented in this book, and it exceeded our expectations. Not only was it an efficient planning tool, it was inclusive, engaging, flexible, and adaptable. It was also fun and inspiring! How many hospital meetings achieve that?"

– Karen Buhler, Department of Family Practice,
British Columbia Women's Hospital

"This book is excellent! It is an essential read for anyone looking to accomplish extraordinary results. The authors do an excellent job explaining what SOAR is and how to use it in any strategic situation that brings out the best possibilities. We use SOAR with clients and have seen its effect on transforming dull strategic planning sessions into engaging and motivating ones!"

– Dr. Fadi Baradihi, Certified Business and Executive Coach,
Baradihi Business Performance

"SOAR is an excellent framework for engaging your organization – moving strategy from formulation to execution. Jackie and Gina have given us an inspirational, yet practical framework for helping leaders engage people in creating strategies. A short read and a must read for those interested in creating strategies and strategic plans that live beyond the annual planning meeting."

– Mona A. Amodeo, Ph.D., Founder and President, idgroup

"In this book, we see that SOAR's use has grown beyond its original intention, helping us to discover innovations in a variety of different areas. All of us dealing with change will be inspired with the thinking behind SOAR – and the practical ways to use it. This book is an invitation to help your team, organization, community, and even yourself move in a direction to achieve aspirations and results!"

– Joep C. de Jong, Founder and CEO of JLS International BV

"*Learning to SOAR* offers an inspired way to see possibility and imagine new solutions. SOAR leverages the strengths inherent in organizations and provides a framework to guide the best in collaborative thinking for improved performance at any level."

– Deborah Maher, President, DFM Consulting

Contents

What you are going to read

This book is about a profoundly positive approach to strategic thinking, planning, and leading that allows any person at any level in any organization to create strategy and strategic plans through shared conversations, collaboration, and a commitment to action. This approach is represented by the acronym SOAR, which stands for:

Strengths: *What are we great at?*

Opportunities: *What are the possibilities?*

Aspirations: *What are our dreams or wishes?*

Results: *What are meaningful outcomes?*

Over the last decade, we have learned from our work and research, as well as from other SOAR practitioners, that conversations about strengths, opportunities, aspirations, and results build trust and positive connections, create innovations, fuel productivity, inspire action, and generate positive change. SOAR has helped individuals, teams, and entrepreneurs in for-profit, non-profit, government, and Fortune 500 organizations. We have experienced or heard of SOAR applications on every continent except Antarctica, in a wide variety of industries from healthcare, education, and government to automotive, hi-tech, retail, service, and manufacturing.

SOAR is distinguished from traditional strategic planning approaches due to its generative nature[1] and the inclusion of stakeholders. Generative conversations create a positive frame for individuals, organizations, and communities[2] because they produce new perspectives, creativity, and ideas.[3] They inspire and move people forward with curiosity, imagination, and engagement. Stakeholders are those people who have a *stake* in the organization's success – employees, board members, customers, suppliers, and the communities where the organization resides. While every stakeholder may not be able to participate in the conversations, each stakeholder group is invited to send a representative.

We have learned that SOAR-based strategic conversations shape a positive frame for strategic direction, plans, innovations, leadership, day-to-day operations, and the well-being of an organization and its stakeholders. David Cooperrider observed that "our organizational lives and the lives of others flourish or flounder one conversation at a time."[4] SOAR's approach to strategic thinking, planning, and leading engages stakeholders in conversations that:

- Identify and build on strengths.
- Connect to and clarify the organization's value set, vision, and mission.
- Discover profitable opportunities such as new markets or innovations that the organization aspires to pursue.
- Determine and align organizational goals and objectives.
- Revise or create new strategies, processes, structures, and systems to support the vision, mission, and goals.
- Implement the strategy or strategic plan so it guides every day decision making and actions.

We understand that organizational leaders and stakeholders face more uncertainty and complexity now than *before*. The before refers to three years or three months or even three minutes ago, because we believe that the amount and speed of uncertainty and complexity are increasing. Today's global workforce operates on a 24-hour, seven-day work week. SOAR can help ensure that each stakeholder has the confidence, knowledge, and skills to act in ways aligned with the organization's values, vision, mission, goals, strategies, and action plans. This book is designed to introduce you to SOAR as a framework to help you, your teams, and organization cope and thrive with increasing change.

Employees want both success and significance. They join organizations to achieve goals they could not accomplish as individuals. They want to engage their minds, hearts, purpose, and spirit in work that is seen as important. They stay with organizations that understand that productivity and engagement are not just tied to wages and financial results but also to recognition, learning, and the ability to make a positive difference. The SOAR framework connects the dots between those individual values and purpose and organization's values, purpose, and vision.

The Thin Book of SOAR introduced SOAR primarily as a strategic thinking and planning framework that can be used in small group strategy conversations and in large group, organization-wide strategic planning and change initiatives. Since its publication, we have experienced immense pride and gratitude to learn of the excellent work done by other practitioners and academics. SOAR is now used at every level, from creating strategy for oneself, to team-based coaching, to strategic conversations at local, national, and international levels in planning and innovation summits. This book shares many of these new examples. We also include several exciting uses of SOAR we had not anticipated. These uses at multiple levels are explored in chapter six. We continue to focus on practical applications that will help you use SOAR to develop a future course of action or project at any level and see how it generates the energy to execute the plan.

Much of what was provided in the seminal writings about the meaning and understanding of SOAR is as true today as it was ten years ago. This book builds upon that foundation and adds:

• Updated stories, case studies, and SOAR snapshots.
• Current research and updated sources.
• Enhanced practical tools, process, and methods like the 5 Is and
  Walk-the-Diamond with updated visuals.
• An exploration of SOAR at additional levels: division, department (function or
  operations), project, team, and individual coaching.

We address the what, why, how, and who of SOAR so that by the end, we hope you understand the core elements and have the confidence to try SOAR or to expand the way you've already used it.

This book is *not* a text on strategy, *nor* is it a deep understanding of strategic planning needed to use SOAR. However, we do provide a list of our favorite strategy books at the end to supplement your growth and knowledge. For now, we invite you to SOAR! We welcome your feedback as you let us know how it goes.

— *Jackie and Gina*

Chapter 1 / **DEFINING SOAR**

... live with uncertainty but act with confidence.
— *Dewitt Jones* [5]

SOAR is a strategic thinking, planning, and leading framework that focuses on strengths, opportunities, aspirations, and results. Focusing on *strengths* means that strategic conversations start with addressing what an individual, team, department, or organization is doing well. Strengths conversations explore what capabilities could be enhanced and what is compelling to those who have a *stake* in the organization's success. The second conversation is about *opportunities* to determine what are possibilities: new ideas, markets, products, services, and other innovations. The third conversation creates shared images – a vision of a future based on *aspirations*. This conversation centers on what might be and identifies which aspirations have the greatest potential to enable the vision to become a reality. The final conversation is about *results*; how will we know when we are succeeding and making a positive difference? What are the meaningful outcomes?

The SOAR approach is also distinguished by the inclusion of a wide variety of stakeholders as a way to understand the *whole system*. The idea is to create a more complete picture of an organization by accessing many different perspectives. One way SOAR does this is to reach beyond senior management to include others in the organization's conversations about strategy.

These stakeholders can be employees from the various parts of the organization, shareholders, customers, board members, suppliers, business partners, volunteers, and community representatives. You can start with internal stakeholders such as employees who are not typically invited into strategic conversations or planning sessions. It is especially important to invite those frontline employees closest to creating the product or providing the service to your customers. The whole system approach tries to understand the dynamics of the many relationships and interactions among people, locations, and functions. This is opposed to viewing an organization as a machine with interchangeable and discrete parts. The whole system approach helps stakeholders see and understand how the system works and where their unique contributions make a difference.

Appreciative is adding valuing and being grateful. Inquiry is about curiosity, wondering, and searching.

Life-giving forces are those elements within an organization that represent its strengths when it is operating at its very best.[6] Aspiration is a strong desire or hope, longing or aim, or a value.

The SOAR framework leverages and integrates *Appreciative Inquiry* (AI) to create a transformational process through positive framing and generative questions. AI is a philosophy and organizational change approach that builds on the strengths and what are called the *life-giving forces* of the organization's existence. David Cooperrider and his colleagues at Case Western Reserve University developed AI in the 1980s. AI engages the whole system in shaping the organization's future by creating a dialogue among stakeholders on *what works* and *how to do more of what works* instead of the traditional diagnostic model of identifying and eliminating problems and gaps. A key appreciative question is 'What is working around here?'[7] AI invites us to discover, dream, and design our destiny to create our most positive and possible future. AI, like SOAR, starts with an intentional discovery of the best in people, teams, organizations, and communities by inquiring into strengths, possibilities, and successes. AI is grounded in the notion that we create each moment, and ultimately our social systems, through conversation and shared meaning-making.[8] AI is one of the most widely used approaches for fostering positive change from the individual to small groups, large organizations, governments, and communities.[9]

SOAR leverages the two AI practices of positive framing and generative questions to guide strategic thinking and conversations. Additionally, SOAR offers a flexible framework that includes the whole system or its representation instead of a more traditional top-down or senior management-only process. What worked in the more hierarchical (and stable) world of the past was top-down strategic direction and planning. However, to deliver innovation and respond to daily challenges, it is critical to engage all levels of stakeholder perspectives and ideas on an on-going basis. The shift needed to gain stakeholder involvement is to connect strategic planning to participants' aspirations, values, and daily work. SOAR does this well. According to a *McKinsey Quarterly* survey of global executives, the highest performing organizations have a clear purpose, an understanding of *strengths*, shared *aspirations*, and leaders who know how to unleash ideas (*opportunities*) with a *results*-driven process.[10]

SOAR invites employees (and other stakeholders) to have a strategic conversation that is grounded in values, strengths, purpose, vision, and action. As a result, employees are motivated by the strategic initiatives that they helped create rather than merely convinced to buy in to what a group at the top envisioned. The division and department goals flow into initiatives and projects that become the basis for individual and team performance plans. *The outcome is clarity, aligned action, and innovation for each stakeholder.*

We have repeatedly experienced how goals are achieved more quickly once this connection and alignment are made. This allows for increased energy and momentum to deal with challenges and potential barriers in real-time. The stakeholders are committed to making a difference because they see how their values and purpose connect with the organization's values and purpose. There is widespread understanding of how the collective effort of the whole system moves the organization forward and benefits all stakeholders. This maximizes people's commitment to contribute their insights and hard work with passion and engagement.

Both AI and SOAR have been utilized by for-profit, non-profit, school systems, governments, professional service organizations, universities, and communities around the world including such organizations as: Clarke, Dell, Facebook, Proctor & Gamble, Boeing, Deere, Google, Target, Marriott International, CareerBuilder, Groupon, McDonalds, Merieux NutriSciences, Flourishing Leadership Institute,

Front Row Foundation, General Motors, Quantum Leap Mastermind, Opioid Crisis Response Workgroup, and the U.S. Army. Even organizations that have long histories and traditions embrace new approaches to sustain their values of innovation, integrity, quality, and commitment. An example where AI and SOAR have been used for more than a decade is John Deere.

SOAR at John Deere

John Deere has been using SOAR at multiple levels since 2003. Deere uses SOAR across and down several divisions and departments (both functional and operations) and as a result links different areas and levels to the overall strategic plan. This helps each employee translate and define his or her action plan and implement it with increased energy, productivity, and willingness to carry out the plans that they helped develop. What especially engages Deere employees is the inquiry into *aspirations* which, in turn, inspires innovation and action based on employees' values and strengths.

SOAR is used to communicate *sustainable value* within organizations. Sustainable value means that an organization considers how its core business impacts the planet and people while making a profit.[11] Deere does this by providing its customers with technologies that encourage effective stewardship of the earth. For example, the information technology used on Deere equipment, maps the land in order to optimize the application of fertilizers, herbicides, and pesticides.

The SOAR approach nurtures a culture of continuous organizational learning because multiple stakeholders participate in SOAR-based strategic conversations and planning sessions. At the division level, participation occurs two to three levels deep, so they learn from each other and establish collaborative working relationships. **Organizational members share and create knowledge and learn how to operate through strategic conversations.** The result is the ability to make decisions in the moment of providing service that align to the organization's purpose, strategy, and goals.

In summary, SOAR increases understanding of how stakeholder efforts fit within the organization's values, mission, vision, goals, and objectives. A strategic plan is dynamic. It can adapt quickly to a changing environment if stakeholders are engaged in the identification of the organization's strengths and opportunities and are constantly scanning the environment for new ones. Everyone at every level can make informed adjustments to decisions and actions when needed. This stakeholder commitment can be the difference between achieving the organization's goals or missing the moving mark.

Now that we know something about SOAR, we can turn our attention in the next chapter to show how a classic strategic analysis tool called SWOT is compared and contrasted with SOAR.

Key Points of this Chapter
- How SOAR relates to Appreciative Inquiry.
- The adaptable nature of SOAR to fit into any strategic conversations or strategic planning process.
- How SOAR supports strategic implementation through the alignment and engagement of stakeholders in strategic thinking, planning, and conversations.

Strategic Questions
- Think about a time when your organization was most successful in adopting a strategy. How important was stakeholder alignment and engagement? Or, how important might it be?
- If you were to use SOAR for a strategy session or to create a strategic plan, who are the relevant stakeholders that you would want to include in the conversation?
- How might you start a strategic conversation that allows for stakeholders' aspirations to be heard?

Chapter 2 / **WHAT IS DIFFERENT ABOUT SOAR?**

The task of leadership is to create an alignment of strengths,
making our weaknesses irrelevant.

— *Peter Drucker*

A standard tool of strategic planning used for decades is called SWOT analysis. SWOT stands for Strengths, Weaknesses, Opportunities, and Threats. SOAR is a framework that guides conversations about strategy formulation and strategic planning as it relates to Strengths, Opportunities, Aspirations, and Results. In this chapter, we compare and contrast SWOT and SOAR, so you begin to understand what is different about SOAR. Although SWOT can be used at any level in an organization, it is traditionally used at the senior leadership level. SOAR is also used at the top level in an organization but seeks to include stakeholders at many levels. This is a key difference because SOAR engages stakeholders who have not traditionally been included in the strategic planning process and who may offer valuable insights.

People frequently ask, 'Is SWOT better than SOAR?' or 'Do I need SWOT if I'm using SOAR?' You can use both if they each serve the strategic needs of the organization. SWOT focuses on diagnostic assessment and analysis. SOAR focuses on dialogue and planning that builds upon the strengths and opportunities from SWOT as a foundation. SOAR then explores aspirations and results. The table on the next page shows the both/and relationship of SWOT and SOAR.

Because many are already familiar with SWOT, this chapter explains how SOAR differs, and how you might consider applying SOAR.[12] The table on page 16 provides another view of the differences between a SWOT Analysis and SOAR Framework.

Comparison of SWOT / SOAR Approaches: *Both / And*

SWOT

STRENGTHS

- Diagnostic assessment and analysis of an organization's resources and capabilities
- Basis for developing differentiating advantage

WEAKNESSES

- Absence of strength; lack of resource or capability
- Flipside of a strength; downside of focusing on competitive advantage

OPPORTUNITIES

- External circumstances (e.g. a trend) that support profit and growth
- Unfulfilled customer needs, new technology, favorable legislation

THREATS

- External circumstances that hinders profit and growth

  E.g., more competitors, changes to revenue stream, restrictive regulations

SOAR

STRENGTHS

- Strategic conversations on: What are we doing really well? What are our greatest assets? What are we most proud of accomplishing? What do our strengths tell us about our skills?
- Basis for developing a strategic advantage

OPPORTUNITIES

- What are possibilities? New ideas, innovations?
- How can we reframe to see opportunities?
- What is the industry or our stakeholders asking us to do? What else may we do?
- How can we best partner with others?
- How do we collectively understand outside threats and create innovative ideas?

ASPIRATIONS

- Considering strengths and opportunities, what are our dreams and wishes? What's compelling?
- How do we allow our values to drive our vision and serve our purpose (mission)?
- How can we make a difference for our organization and its stakeholders?

RESULTS

- What are our measurable and meaningful outcomes?
- What do we want to be known for?
- How do we tangibly translate strengths, opportunities, and aspirations?

SWOT ANALYSIS	SOAR FRAMEWORK
Analysis oriented: Focus on diagnostic assessment	Action oriented: Focus on strategic conversations
Competition focus – Just be better	Possibility focus – Be the best!
Incremental improvement	Innovation and breakthroughs
Top down	Engagement of all levels
Focus on analysis → planning	Focus on planning → implementation
Energy depleting – *There are so many weaknesses and threats!*	Energy creating – *We are good and can become great!*
Attention to gaps	Attention to results

Another key distinction of SOAR is to identify and expand existing strengths and opportunities rather than drill down on problems, deficiencies, weaknesses, and threats. Dedicating the same amount of time to each of the four SWOT components means spending half the time thinking about positives (strengths and opportunities) and the other half thinking about negatives (weaknesses and threats). This effort limits forward momentum. There is research to support that building on people's strengths can produce greater results than spending time on correcting their weaknesses.[13]

People tend to look for problems and focus on weakness and threats before searching for possibilities. For example, one participant of a SWOT process described this tendency as follows: "Having used SWOT analysis for the previous 15 years, I had experienced that it could be draining, as people often got stuck in the weaknesses and threats conversations. The analysis became a negative spiral of energy." Or, as another described his experience of a planning process deeply rooted in a SWOT analysis, "[the SWOT approach] gave us a plan but took our spirit."[14] From our experience, drained energy and loss of spirit can negatively impact momentum and achieving results.

In SOAR, we explore strengths and opportunities so that we can align and expand them until they lessen or manage weaknesses and threats. **Weaknesses** and threats are not ignored. They are reframed and given the appropriate focus within the opportunities and results conversation. Ultimately, it becomes a question of balance. Why not spend as much time or more on what you do well and how you can do *more* of that? What gives you more energy to act? What gives you confidence to set a stretch goal?

The Research

Research confirms what we knew intuitively – energy focused on strengths and opportunities promotes successful individual and team performance in organizations. It increases productivity 1.5 times greater than a focus on weaknesses and threats.[15] Research also shows that a focus on strengths promotes positive emotions and upward spirals toward optimal individual and organizational performance. Dr. Barbara Fredrickson's research in this area, described in her book *Positivity*, concludes we are three times more likely to achieve optimal levels of well-being when we experience positive rather than negative emotions. She defines ten forms of positive emotions that characterize a positive state of mind[16] including joy, hope, interest, inspiration and amusement.

Adding to Fredrickson's work are the years of research by her colleagues, Dr. Marcial Losada and Dr. Emily Heaphy, analyzing how people talk to each other in team meetings. They coded and sorted conversations into a mathematical model that plots significant differences between three categories: positive or negative, other-focused or self-focused, and asking questions or defending a point of view. Those differences were subsequently mapped onto team performance. High performing teams are six times more likely to have conversations with positive emotions, were other-focused, and asked more questions.[17] These are also the characteristics of SOAR's strategic conversations. SOAR is a way to help people experience these best practices so teams can thrive and flourish.

Citing from a wide range of research and real-world examples, Kim Cameron reports that high-levels of meaningfulness in work have been associated with positive outcomes and extraordinary individual and organizational performance.[18] In a powerful example from his research with Marc Lavine, *Making the Impossible Possible*, he describes an effort to clean up a contaminated nuclear plant. The job was completed 60 years earlier than scheduled, $30 billion under budget, and 13 times cleaner than mandated. Over the years, the stakeholders worked together, the once contentious relationships changed to become positive. Cameron attributes this to a shared moral purpose and years of collaboration that transformed this dangerous site to "a wildlife refuge – a safe environment for thousands of years to come."[19]

What we have learned since our first writing is that the research on positivity in leadership correlates with an individual's or team's capacity for collaboration and high performance. This upward spiral improves individual and organizational health. There are reductions in stress, turnover, absenteeism, dissatisfaction, and cynicism, as well as increases in commitment, innovation, engagement, empowerment, satisfaction, and a sense of fulfillment.[20] SOAR helps people connect and align their values and purpose to their work through the strategic conversations about the organization's values, vision, and mission.

We believe that strategy should be a living, energy-creating part of everyone's job. Many of us may have had the experience of being presented with a strategic plan that we were expected to implement, despite our lack of input into the plan. **What is different about SOAR is it engages stakeholders from all levels to contribute their ideas.** Because of this participation, it has been our experience that implementation time is significantly reduced. In the following example, we will show you how strategy became part of everyone's job in the organization.

Learning to SOAR: From Average to Top-Performance

A regional office of a global professional services firm used SOAR to engage all its employees and a few key customers. What follows are the impressive results. Prior to using SOAR, the office was holding its own in its global ranking and was known as an average performing office. It ranked 8th in total revenues and 12th out of 25 offices in operating profit. In addition, employee engagement and retention rates were low. With an annualized employee turnover rate of 36%, the office ranked 6th in the firm for retaining employees. The office was meeting expectations, but the leadership team believed it could do better.

The strategic planning team decided to integrate the SOAR framework by first including a group of 40 internal stakeholders that represented the various positions in the organization. Within the next few months, all employees were invited into the process. The managing director thought that building on what the firm was doing well and then engaging all the employees in a strategic conversation would yield a positive impact on meeting client satisfaction, operations, and financial goals. From the SOAR sessions, leadership and team meetings, client interviews, and cross-functional meetings, the leadership team created a three-year strategic plan based on the information summarized in the table below. The Executive Director recalled "while the plan was being written, everyone was inspired to take action." This was demonstrated in the first year as employee engagement improved significantly. The office moved to being ranked first in engagement. From continued implementation in years two to four, the office became the firm's largest and most profitable operation, ranking first in employee engagement, retention, client satisfaction, revenue, and income. The employee turnover rate decreased from 36% to just 7%.

	STRENGTHS	OPPORTUNITIES
STRATEGIC INQUIRY	• Deep client perception of value creation and reference support • Strong professional relationships • Committed and competent leadership team • Professional workforce desiring growth, learning, and relationships	• Significantly grow accounts that have most potential • Improve profitability margins • Adapt organizational structure to support continued growth with rewards • Team and workforce development
APPRECIATIVE INTENT	**ASPIRATIONS** • To be recognized trusted advisor to clients • Serve 60% of companies with over $1 billion in revenues • Be in the top decile of the firm in measures of client satisfaction, employee engagement, employee retention, profitability, and revenue • Best serve our team and clients so we are Practice of the Year	**RESULTS** / measurements • Earn client satisfaction of no less than 3.5 on a scale of 4.0 • Add to large clients (capability of over $5 million in revenue) and increase total revenues by 20% • Improve net profit margin by 8% • Achieve employee engagement score above 90% and employee turnover below 12%

Relative Rank of the Office within the Firm

	YEAR 1		YEAR 2	YEAR 3	YEAR 4
Employee Engagement	6th	**S**	1st	1st	1st
Employee Retention	6th	**O**	3rd	1st	1st
Client Satisfaction	8th	**A**	8th	6th	1st
Revenue	8th	**R**	5th	4th	1st
Income	12th		6th	2nd	1st

Source: Chapter 18, Linking Strategy and OD to Sustainable Performance by Stavros, J. and Saint, D. in W. Rothwell, J. Stavros, R. Sullivan, and A. Sullivan in Practicing Organization Development: A Guide to Leading Change, 2010, Jossey-Bass.

SOAR provides those responsible for strategic planning the framework to engage internal and external stakeholders in conversations about what is going well in the organization and what is possible. This is an open invitation to surface innovations in products and services, structure, process, and methods. As the strategic planning process unfolds, there is implementation with inspiration. How can you achieve those results and make strategy part of everyone's job? The next two chapters provide details on how to get started.

Key Points of this Chapter
• Compares and differentiates SOAR from SWOT.
• Provides research from social sciences.
• Shows the possibility focus of using SOAR to create greater innovation and energy for change.

Strategic Questions
• Is your organization directing energy on weaknesses and deficits or on strengths and possibilities?
• How can SOAR be applied at the top levels of the organization or for cascading and aligning to other levels?
• Review the questions in the SWOT and SOAR diagram. How would you rephrase the questions to fit your strategic planning conversations?
• How might you reframe a weakness or threat into a possibility, aspiration, or future opportunity that inspires?

Chapter 3 / **WHAT IS THE ESSENCE OF SOAR?**

Within our dreams and aspirations, we find our opportunities.
— *Sue Atchley Ebaugh*

SOAR initiates a series of *conversations* to help everyone gain a whole system perspective. This happens by involving those who are connected to each other by that system, including frontline employees, customers, suppliers, business partners, volunteers, regulators, and community representatives. Participants are encouraged "to think about the organization as a system whose parts are mutually interdependent."[21] The SOAR conversations are designed to help the organization's stakeholders understand what happens when the organization is working at its best, explore what is possible, and how to apply that information to create a desired future, with defined results.

SOAR Questions

SOAR differs from other strategic approaches because of the inclusive nature of the conversations. Here are samples of questions used in SOAR conversations. For each conversation, we offer a basic question that is italicized and several supporting questions. This gives you an example of the type of questions you can ask stakeholders. You can also adapt the questions depending on the application and language you are most comfortable using. The questions should be reviewed with the session leaders or a core strategic planning team.

Strengths: *What are we great at?*

What are we most proud of as an organization (division, department)?

How does that reflect our greatest strength?

What makes us unique? From this, what can we build on?

What is our proudest achievement in the last year or two?

How do we leverage our strengths to get results?

How do our strengths fit with the realities of the marketplace?

What do we do or provide that is world class for our customers, our industry, and other potential stakeholders?

Opportunities: *What are the possibilities?*

How do we make sense of opportunities based on external forces and trends?

What are the top three opportunities on which we should focus our efforts?

How might we best meet the needs of our stakeholders, including customers, employees, shareholders, and community?

Who are possible new customers?

How can we distinctively differentiate ourselves from existing or potential competitors?

What are possible new markets, products, services, or processes?

How can we reframe challenges to be seen as exciting opportunities?

What new skills do we need to move forward?

Aspirations: *What are our dreams or wishes?*

What do we care deeply about?

What can we be best at in our world? [22]

Reflecting on strengths and opportunities conversations: who are we, who should we become, and where should we go in the future?

What is our most compelling aspiration?

What strategic initiatives (i.e. projects, programs, and processes) would support our aspirations?

Results: *What are meaningful outcomes?*

Considering our strengths, opportunities, and aspirations: what meaningful measure would indicate that we are on track to achieving our goals and meeting objectives?

What are three to five indicators that would create a scorecard that addresses a triple bottom line of profit, people, and planet?

How do we know we are making a difference? Succeeding? Completing strategic initiatives?

What resources are needed to implement our most vital projects?

What are the best rewards to support those who achieve our goals?

The questions are the basis for conversations first held in small groups. This is followed by reporting out to a larger group to create shared understanding. The small group to large group conversation flow works because participants have a sense of safety and a greater chance to contribute their knowledge and thoughts in the small group. By reporting to the large group, shared thinking and critical mass are created. This approach shows how SOAR is scalable (small to large group) and shows how SOAR conversations can be beneficial at any level in the organization or community. They can involve any number of participants in the same physical location or connected virtually.

Conventional wisdom holds that the most effective size for strategic planning teams is seven to 12 participants from the top levels of the firm. We would like to disrupt convention. Larger groups, with participants at many levels, can be engaged with small group breakout sessions and collaborative technology. There is no limit to the participant size of a strategic planning session. Using SOAR and the small to large group approach, it is possible to have effective sessions with groups that exceed even 1000 people! With the help of web-enabled technology, participants can be anywhere in the world, increasing knowledge and commitment across global organizations and significantly reducing implementation time.[23]

For example, ten years ago, Northern Essex Community College (NECC), which has multiple campuses in the Boston area, initially engaged a core strategic planning team of 20 people. The interest in serving on this team was so overwhelmingly positive, that the college decided to be as inclusive as possible and opened team membership to any and all interested stakeholders. As a result, another 25 people joined the strategic planning team. By the time the two-day regional planning forum was held, over 170 stakeholders participated, including students, alumni, parents, administrators, faculty, staff, board of trustees, and community supporters. The outcome of this relatively brief event was a three-year strategic plan with a core value set, a clear vision, a mission, and six strategic initiatives and measures to lead the college from a no-growth to a growth strategy throughout the entire region.[24]

For NECC, the SOAR Strategic Planning Summit helped to guide a productive and efficient strategic planning forum. They embedded Appreciative Inquiry and SOAR in their culture from professional development, team building, alumni groups, academic master plans, and even in the classroom. Post-summit, NECC demonstrated its growth as a learning organization by holding 32 SOAR forums with over 310 participants including 100 students that resulted in five strategic directions: support success, strengthen community, respect diversity, foster leadership, and maximize resources.[25]

In Chapter 4 and 5, you will learn how to take the SOAR framework and use it within what we call the 5-I Cycle. Next, we show two Quick SOAR examples.

Quick SOAR

SOAR is scalable. It serves the need to quickly create a strategy for an idea, project, issue, or initiative at any level in an organization or community. A good example from a Canadian Women's Hospital illustrates how SOAR was applied in just three hours to create a working agreement called a compact. Participants in the meeting included the hospital president, the consultant experienced with care-provider hospital compacts, a member of the hospital charitable foundation, and representative midwifery and physician leaders from all parts of the hospital. By the time introductions were completed and the team brought up to date, there were only two hours left in the meeting. They bravely launched into a Quick SOAR. The goals were:

• To explore the forces and factors that give life to the medical/midwifery staff in their work at Women's Hospital.

• To design the framework for a process to create a compact between care-providers and the hospital that helps the whole organization become the best it can be.

• To provide an experience of SOAR for the leadership team so that they could evaluate if SOAR would work well for the overall compact process.

The following questions were asked of the participants:

1. What attracted you to our hospital?

2. Describe a high point experience at our hospital. This is a time when you felt most alive, most engaged and most proud of your involvement. What are the strengths we can build upon?

3. Envision a time in the future when there is complete and exciting engagement of all the physicians and midwives here. What would it be like to work in this place? What new innovations have occurred? How might this help our hospital to be the best it can be?

4. As you think about the larger context and purpose of our hospital, what are the most important aspirations that would result from a fully engaged medical and midwifery staff?

5. In designing a process for a compact, what are the top three to five indicators that will make it successful? How do we know we are succeeding (results)?

The SOAR interviews took 30-minutes per pair (15-minutes per person). Then, each table had a 15-minute dialogue on strengths, a 30-minute visioning exercise, and a 15-minute opportunities dialogue. With 30-minutes left, as the group reported out, the facilitators organized data into shared strengths, visions, and opportunities with closing thoughts of indicators of success (results). At the end of the meeting, there was a clear idea of how to proceed with the project, and all participants were happy with both the process and end product. Even though this meeting occurred at night after a full-day's work for everyone, they felt invigorated. There were also a few surprises. According to the facilitator, the first was how well the Quick SOAR went. The participants reported that the questions were very helpful to guide the conversation. Second, they discovered that SOAR innately produces engagement by creating an opportunity for dialogue, deep listening, and a sense of community and valued participation. Third, participants were amazed at the efficiency of SOAR. By starting from strengths and success and taking the time to create shared visions before brainstorming opportunities, the practical results and solutions seemed to fall into place. Lastly, they had fun and were inspired.[26]

The wide variety in the number of participants impacts the time it takes to answer the SOAR questions so there isn't any standard way or schedule. We have conducted many half-day to full-day sessions that we refer to as Quick SOAR. For a Quick SOAR session, the small group conversations can be scheduled allowing 30 to 60 minutes of dialogue and 15 to 20 minutes for report out on each of the four SOAR elements. A sample schedule is at the end of the chapter. No matter how much time you have available, the goal is to ensure all participants are heard. Also, there needs to be sufficient information and time to support an inquiry, imagine what might be, and make informed decisions to move ahead with a strategy, a tactical plan, or next steps in a strategy conversation to achieve results.

Here's one more example by a director of a task force in an inner city who needed a strategy to create a youth leadership development program that inspired open dialogue, diversity, and inclusion to obtain funding for the program. The director held a five-hour strategic conversation using a slight adaptation of the main SOAR questions listed in this chapter. The questions and summary of answers are shown on the next page.

Strengths: *What have we done well? What can we build on?*
Community presence in inner city and 10-mile radius
Peace walk celebrations
Youth peacemakers
Taskforce diversity
Young members and adult members blend
Attract leaders to speak to members

Opportunities: *What can we do for our youth?*
Create a youth leadership program that advances our legacy
Partner with local and national youth groups
Send youths to presidential inaugurations
Leverage leadership team to design the best youth leadership program in the nation

Aspirations: *What do we desire to be?*
To be the premier catalysts for outreach to communities and their youth to develop leadership programs through our legacy of positive social change, equality, diversity, and education.

Results: *How do we know we are succeeding?*
Funding is received for the Youth Legacy Leadership Development Program.
A vibrant and meaningful youth leadership program is created.
Youth are accepted from all over the city and there is a waiting list for next year's program. Abundance of leaders are applying to teach, mentor, coach our youths into effective leaders.

From this Quick SOAR session, held in just five hours with 14 participants, the director created a proposal for funding the leadership development program. Within three months, the funding was received to develop the program. Four months after that, several youths attended a Presidential Inauguration in Washington, D.C.

The scalability of SOAR allows the framework to be applied from a Quick SOAR to a more rigorous and formal two to three-day strategic planning event. A Quick SOAR is especially suited to divisional, departmental, project, and individual short-term tactical planning where alignment to the larger organization's strategy is critical (See Chapter 6).

When a more rigorous and formal SOAR-based strategic planning method is called for we use a 5-I Cycle (Initiate, Inspire, Imagine, Innovate, and Implement).

Key Points of this Chapter
- Provided examples of SOAR-based questions.
- Provided illustrations of a Quick SOAR process and output.

Strategic Questions
- What are key SOAR questions that you might ask at your next planning meeting to start a conversation that aims to build a strategy or strategic plan?
- What is a possible Quick SOAR application?

Quick SOAR Sample Agenda

MINS	PARTICIPANTS	TOPIC / DISCUSSION	COMMENTS /METHOD
30	Facilitator & All	Strengths introduction & breakout	5 min intro, 25 min discussion
40	Teams	Strengths conversation and report outs	5 mins per team/ table. 50 participants
5	Facilitator & All	Strengths debrief	What did we learn? What does it mean? What will we do about it?
15	Sr Leader	Opportunity knowledge leveling	Sr. leader gives insight into trends, issues, forces. Presentation & discussion
30	Teams	Opportunity conversation	Team identifies opportunities, adds insights. Reframes challenges.
40	Teams & Facilitator	Report out & opportunity mapping	5 min per team/table. 50 participants @ 7 tables = 35 min
5	Teams	Opportunity debrief	What does it mean, what will we do?
30	Facilitator & All	Aspirations introduction & breakout	5 min intro, 25 min group
45	LUNCH BREAK		
40	Teams	Aspirations conversation & report outs	5 min per team (table). 50 participants
40	Facilitator & All	Aspirations debrief	What did we learn, what does it mean, what will we do?
30	Facilitator & All	Results introduction and breakout	Introduce results breakout (5 min), small group
40	Teams	Results report outs	5 minutes per team/table. 50 participants @ 7 tables = 35 min
40	Facilitator & All	Results debrief	What did we learn, what does it mean, what will we do about it?

Chapter 4 / **HOW TO SOAR WITHIN THE 5-I'S**

We will either find a way, or make one.

— Hannibal

Initiate
Choosing to SOAR

Inquire
Asking the SOAR questions

SOAR

Implement
Moving to inspired action

Imagine
Creating a shared vision

Innovate
Designing the strategic initiatives

Through our practice with SOAR, we have used a 5-I Cycle to take a whole system approach in creating a strategic plan. This chapter is *how to do* SOAR through the 5-I Cycle of Initiate, Inquire Imagine, Innovate, and Implement phases. We want to emphasize that there is no one right way to SOAR. It is a scalable and flexible framework used to create strategies and strategic plans. Whichever strategic method you use to apply SOAR, the goal is to make it inclusive and built from the best representation of stakeholders possible. This chapter provides an illustration of how an HR Function used the 5-I Cycle in their organization's strategic initiative to create a plan to Go Global.

Initiate: Choosing to SOAR

During the Initiate phase, leadership determines the efficacy of using SOAR and intentionally designs the engagement. The following are typical steps:

• Create a core planning team. These are individuals who can be involved in design and delivery of the 5-I Cycle using SOAR. This team provides the strategic vision into what they want to achieve.

• Identify the type and number of stakeholders needed to gain a whole system perspective.

• Determine when and how the stakeholders can be engaged. Plan how you will gather the stakeholders and information to provide clarity for the initiative/ project plan. Will it be a one-day strategic conversation to create a strategy (at what level?) or a two to three-day large group strategic planning summit? If some stakeholders cannot attend the scheduled session, how can their perspectives be included in the plan? What choices and constraints need to be defined and communicated?

• Craft the questions to ask the participant stakeholders.

The Human Resource (HR) function of a global Fortune 100 company needed to respond to the corporate strategy for global growth and high-performance teamwork. HR's leadership team decided to use SOAR within a 5-I Cycle since they needed innovation and engagement for the potential of a great deal of structural change. A core planning team first used SOAR to develop a charter to re-organize HR into a truly global function. A large group summit would be used to execute the remaining 4-I phases. A facilitator was engaged to work with the leadership and core team to develop the following project and summit questions:[27]

- How have prior strategic plans been created and executed? Is there a need for greater alignment, engagement, and innovation?
- What does being global really mean? What should we keep, extend, and/or stop doing within the HR function to be global?
- Who are the stakeholders that should be directly involved in the global HR strategy planning process? How do we make sure all stakeholders are represented in the conversation? How do we communicate their involvement?
- What are the project team's strengths and experience in strategic execution?
- What do we hope to gain from using the SOAR framework?
- When and where do we conduct the global HR initiative conversations?
- What data needs to be readily available for the session?
- How do we provide clarity of the vision, mission, roadmap, and expected results to the stakeholders?

The types of SOAR questions can vary, but the intent of the Initiate phase is to have leadership understand and commit how to use SOAR within the 5-I Cycle. In this phase, the core planning team works out the details of how information will be gathered and who will participate before starting the Inquire phase.

Inquire: Asking the SOAR questions

In this phase, participants attending the strategic planning event engage in one-on-one interviews, then small group table conversations using the SOAR-based questions designed in the Initiate phase. These small group conversations (table teams) are reported out to the whole group and may include: strengths, values, aspirations, opportunities for growth, and/or definitions of success. It includes a report or visual to make sure there is shared knowledge of the topics, project, and the current state. This sharing of themes provides grounding for the entire group and establishes the foundation to launch the next phase – Imagine.

For the global HR initiative, a two-day large group summit included 40 employees who attended in-person and another 15 virtual participants. Senior HR Leadership clarified the purpose and desired outcome of the summit and the global HR project. After the convening and the introduction, a 45-minute Inquire breakout used questions focusing on the S-O of SOAR in small table groups of seven to eight. The questions were adapted to help go beyond past assumptions.

- When have we been at our best collaborating globally to support operations?
- What does being global really mean? What should we keep, extend, and/or stop doing within the HR function to be global?
- What are best practices for global HR functions?

There was a report out to the whole group to achieve collective understanding. The Strengths conversation was a great beginning since HR was often blamed by operations when results were not achieved. The participants took time to reflect on their strengths and the successes achieved in the last two years. This reminded them what they are best at and that they had made significant contributions to the organization. This produced energy and confidence on issues that would be explored in the Opportunities conversation.

To begin the Opportunities inquiry, HR Leadership first shared their view of the enterprise strategy, external trends, and impacts to HR function's goals. This second conversation focused on possibilities for how HR could best support global growth asking, "how might we work together to best support our global strategy?" The observations were made visual on mind-maps[28] and flip charts and then posted so that collective understanding could be built on in the next phase, Imagine.

The size of the group and the questions asked will vary, but the intent of the Inquire phase is to create a collective understanding of the group's strengths and opportunities. This common understanding lets the group use their imagination to consider what might be in the Imagine phase.

Imagine: Creating a shared vision

In this phase, small groups engage in *possibility thinking*. The goal is to imagine what might happen as they go beyond the shared information and insights from the Inquire phase to envision a desired future. Aspirations are at the heart of this conversation. Participants imagine a compelling future. Participants are encouraged to be as creative and innovative as possible to visualize a future that reflects high potential opportunities, strengths, and aspirations of the stakeholders.

The small group to large group conversation flow used in the Inquire phase should be used again. This phase can be accomplished in a short amount of time (one to two hours), since this is intuitive, top of mind, and encourages breakthrough thinking. Facilitators record and collect the ideas and themes from the imagined futures. A consolidated report is made available to the whole group. These tangible images and supporting dialogue create the inspiration and excitement to translate strategic visions into coordinated plans and action in the next phase, Innovate.

For the global HR initiative summit, the Imagine breakout created an environment of fun and creativity. It gave the participants permission to question traditional organization charts. This was done by presenting skits, magazine articles, and graphic visualizations. HR participants went beyond a silo perspective to consider the impact of what they called *Glocal HR* (both Global and local) on their stakeholders, the environment, and profitability of the enterprise. The group found that the Imagine phase engaged the heart, mind, and spirit of the participants and produced excitement and energy for the next two phases.

In the Imagine phase, the facilitator continually reminds the group of the strengths, opportunities, and aspirations, uncovered from the Inquire and Imagine phases. All of this information is used as the foundation for specific strategic initiatives and designs created in the next phase, Innovate.

Innovate: Designing the strategic initiatives

This phase transforms the imaginative ideas from the Inquire and Imagine phases into strategic initiatives and actionable plans. Because every organization has limited resources, priority choices are made based on the best possibilities. To define what is required for the chosen possibilities, we use a design approach called Walk-the-Diamond. This systematically considers whether there is a need to revise design elements such as the business process, organization structure, management systems, or organization culture (see table on page 34: Questions for Design Elements: Walk-the-Diamond). The leadership team needs to make the group aware of available resources as well as encourage conversations about what other resources are needed.

The HR team referred to the Innovate phase as *Get Creative, then Get Real.* The openness of the Imagine phase uncovered multiple possibilities, new paradigms, and a project branded *Glocal HR.* The Innovate phase prioritized those possibilities into the vital few projects that focused on developing HR business processes and a global HR organization structure.

The disciplined approach of *Walk-the-Diamond* offered the questions to get to a project level design and blueprints for action plans. To start, they identified five HR business processes that needed to be reengineered to become truly *Glocal.* The organization structure was reconfigured to a regional, local, and corporate level. The action plans were used in the Implement phase.

Questions for Design Elements: Walk-the-Diamond

DESIGN ELEMENT	QUESTIONS
Process • Work activity flow • Information flow	*Current State:* Where do we have a best practice in this process for delivering value to our customer? What aspects of our current process do we want to make sure we carry forward? *Future State:* What processes do we need to meet our goals of quality, safety, speed, and cost?
Organization Structure • Roles & Responsibilities • Relationships • Locations	*Current State:* What current roles and responsibilities have been especially effective for the organization or process? *Future State:* What would be new roles, responsibilities and/or reporting structures to better support our customers and organization?
Management Systems • Information Systems • Measurement Systems • Budgeting Systems	*Current State:* Where are we most effective in delivering information to those who need it at the time they need it? How can we further deploy any best practices in information or metrics delivery? *Future State:* What would we need to develop to more effectively deliver information/knowledge and/or metrics to the people who need them? How can we best share information and metrics, so everyone can see our progress?
Culture & Behaviors • Subcultures • Stories & Artifacts • Rewards	*Current State:* What can we learn from our organization's stories? What changes need to be made in our culture or subcultures? *Future State:* What culture would reinforce the behavior for what we need to develop in the future?

Implement: Moving to inspired action

Ultimately, plans must be created to realize the designs from the Innovate phase. The Implement phase creates the tactical plans and takes the actions needed to lead to success. The energy and commitment from prior phases create the momentum to inspire the completion of the actions to achieve results. Meaningful and measurable goals are defined, and the results are then visually shared to be used as feedback and course corrections. Implementation involves many stakeholders with different skills collaborating on linked projects.

For *Glocal HR*, the HR processes and organization structure projects were chartered using SOAR conversations. The charters were translated to project management plans including change management plans, objectives, and scoreboards to visibly track the results. They called this *Sustainability through Visibility*. The SOAR framework and 5-I Cycle helped translate innovative ideas and plans into desirable results by implementing the desired change into each employee's Individual Development Plan.

The Implement phase took the design details from the Innovate phase and created projects or action plans to implement the design. Since SOAR is effective in developing project plans, the conversations continued with the stakeholders of the projects. The work required to sustain new strengths and maintain new opportunities is ongoing and iterative. Continuous improvement involves checking back with stakeholders to make sure the aspirations and results continue to be achieved.

What gives the 5-I Cycle so much impact is the original power and inspiration generated by the Inquire and Imagine conversations. Those SOAR conversations thread through the phases connecting everyone to the why and how. Stakeholders are motivated and inspired to focus and invest their energy. The rewards are many: financial returns, an engaged, coordinated and productive workforce, and new thinking. This leads to new products, services, markets, and positive customer experiences that define the organization and provides differentiators.

We want to emphasize that SOAR goes beyond just producing great ideas. SOAR transforms the way people in organizations think and work together. Once organizations open themselves to an inclusive and generative way of working, they are capitalizing on the strengths everyone brings. An upward spiral of positive momentum is created which is self-perpetuating over time. In the next chapter, we will illustrate the SOAR framework and the 5-I Cycle with a case study on creating a strategic plan.

Key Points of this Chapter

- Provided insight and examples of SOAR within the 5-I Cycle to create and implement strategies or strategic, project, or action plans.
- Provided a list of questions to consider when designing the strategic initiatives (Walk-the-Diamond).

Strategic Questions

- How might you introduce SOAR framework and the 5-Is to create a strategic project plan?
- What will people want and need to know before getting started?
- What is the best way to create alignment, innovation, engagement, and energy?

Chapter 5 / **PUTTING IT ALL TOGETHER**

A leader is best when people barely know he exists.
When his work is done, they will say: we did it ourselves.

— *Lao Tzu*

Haverwood Healthcare is a mid-sized regional provider of post-acute services, including nursing homes, assisted living, and rehabilitation services. Each year the company's senior management team sequestered themselves in a hotel to develop the strategic plan for the coming year. During a typical strategic planning session, top management reviewed their prior year's goals, objectives, strategies, plans, and policies from which new goals and objectives would be developed for the coming year. Heavy emphasis was placed on areas where the company missed their budget and financial projections in discussions about what went wrong. This annual ritual centered on a SWOT analysis and setting goals and a budget to support it.

Review the Mission

The traditional first step in this ritual was to review the current strategic position of the organization. It began with a broad overview of the company's financial statements and discussion of the existing mission statement. Haverwood Healthcare's mission statement provided a purpose or function for the organization — the reason for which the organization exists: *We are a quality provider of diversified healthcare services by:*

• *Emphasizing high standards of performance and integrity that will enhance the quality of life of our residents.*

• *Providing our employees opportunities for growth through participation, achievement, recognition, and reward.*

• *Maintaining a strong economic base through sound practices in support of these goals.*

The *mission statement* answers the questions, who are we and what business are we in? A mission statement, which emphasizes the present state of the business, is most effective when developed alongside a *guiding vision statement.* The vision statement answers the question, where do we want to be in the future? The senior management team had created the following vision statement before using SOAR: *To be the long-term healthcare provider of choice in our market areas.*

Review the Goals

The next step in Haverwood Healthcare's strategic planning process was to review existing goals. *Goals* are open-ended statements about such wishes as *being profitable* or *achieving growth in the long-term care market.* In strategic planning language, goals with measures are often called *objectives.* For example, Haverwood Healthcare's objective was to improve bottom line profitability by 20% in five years. This is a quantifiable statement about a desired strategic goal. Next, the senior management team evaluated the effectiveness of strategies. A *strategy* is simply the *how to* or means to achieve objectives. Strategies are often defined by level. For example:

Corporate: Should we grow, maintain status quo, or exit?

Unit: How do we uniquely contribute? What is our competitive advantage? How do we sustain ourselves in the marketplace?

Functional: What should each functional area do to align with the unit and corporate level strategies?

Despite top management's annual strategic planning session and their future looking vision statement, the reality at Haverwood was that senior management rarely thought about the future strategic direction of the company and innovations impacting its 2800 employees, residents (customers), and community stakeholders. The healthcare market is highly dynamic with constantly evolving competitive, environmental, and legislative changes. However, senior management at Haverwood believed they were proficient at reacting to outside stimuli by operating from the assumption that if the daily operations were at a breakeven point, the future would take care of itself. A new CEO and Vice President of Business Development who heard about SOAR and the 5-I Cycle wanted to explore how their traditional strategic planning process could be more inclusive, engaging, and focused on a desired future built on strengths, opportunities, and aspirations of the stakeholders. The following sections describe Haverwood Healthcare's new strategic planning approach using SOAR and the 5-I Cycle.

Initiate: *How shall we work together?*

For years, Haverwood Healthcare had taken a defensive posture in their markets, working hard to maintain a solid footing in the communities in which they operated. Even when a residential healthcare center did not meet the desired vision of being the provider of choice, the company often maintained it. They feared that alternative actions, like closing the facility, might cause more problems. However, during a recent strategic planning session, it became clear that one of the assisted living facilities had been operating at a deficit for three years. It did not meet the company's objective for profitability, nor was it a center of choice. Senior management felt that they had to face the difficult decision of whether to continue investing significant resources in an attempt to turn the center around, sell it, or close it.

A review showed that for the past several years, the center had been steadily losing market share and was currently operating at 75% of bed capacity. This particular assisted living center also had a unionized staff. The staff's attitude towards the center's management team could best be described as tolerant. Further investment in this center would mean less money available for some of Haverwood's more profitable centers. Divestiture could mean loss of market share, stirring up regulatory issues, attracting negative press, angering families and residents, and damaging the company's statewide reputation.

To help analyze the difficult decision of potentially closing a center, the company decided to bring in a consultant team that was familiar with SOAR to develop a facility level strategic plan at this center. Their hope was to facilitate positive change by first bringing the center to a break-even point and then operating it at a profit.

What they liked about the SOAR framework was that it would bring the facility's staff, management, residents, and family members together as a unified team to create a strategic plan at the facility level. They also hoped that the process would help build a positive working culture. Bringing these stakeholders together was important because SOAR would address diverse factors that inhibited the center's growth: management and staff relations, census development (revenue), and resident satisfaction. In many ways, this was a final attempt to get everyone working together toward improving the center's bottom line and reputation while creating the most preferred future.

The consultants *initiated* the strategic planning process by meeting with the center's management team and identifying a core team of people from various stakeholder groups, including management, staff, residents, and family members, who would participate in SOAR-based conversations. Haverwood's Vice-President of Business Development served on the team as the representative of the organization's top management. During the six-week strategic planning process, facilitated by the consultants, this core team would identify and involve relevant stakeholders to develop an appropriate strategy for the struggling center.

Inquire: *What are our strengths and opportunities?*

Once the core planning team was identified, the consultants worked with the team to create the following questions that would become the basis for the Inquire phase:

- Why did you join Haverwood Healthcare? How long have you been with Haverwood Healthcare? What is your role and contribution(s)?
- Describe a rewarding experience or high point during your employment with Haverwood Healthcare. This would be a time when you felt most proud and excited about being part of our organization.
- What is it that you value about yourself, the nature of your work, the people you work with, and the residents?
- When your facility is operating at its best, what are the core *strengths* that give *life* to this center, without which the center would cease to exist?
- What are the *opportunities* for this facility? How can we best serve the residents? What potential do you see? What else is possible?
- What are the *aspirations* of your department? What image do you have for our facility? What would you like our future to look like?
- What are the *results* that we can measure? What results are most meaningful to you? How will we know we have accomplished something?

The core group created a list of the stakeholders and divided them into small groups of three to five people. Then, the above questions were slightly adapted for use with the residents and their family members. Members from the core team met with each small group and used the questions to guide SOAR conversations. During the Inquire phase, particular attention was paid to ensure that all stakeholder groups were represented in an open discussion of the possibility that the facility might be closed or sold.

Because SOAR asks generative questions, the small group interaction tends to create a significant amount of energy, discussion, and collaboration. Generative questions change how people think, feel, and act. These types of questions "make room for diverse and different perspectives, surface new information and knowledge, and stimulate creativity and innovation."[29] The mere act of asking SOAR-based questions began to shift the mind, heart, and attitude of the people. The center's Executive Director commented, "I'm amazed at how willing the staff and residents, plus their family members were to participate and was thrilled with how engaged they became in the conversations. We definitely got off on the right foot. As soon as we started asking questions, they became noticeably more relaxed and quickly started sharing wonderful stories about their experiences (strengths) and possibilities (opportunities) with the center. There is no question that this energy carried us through the remainder of the strategic planning process."

Imagine: *What can we aspire to?*

Next, the findings from the strategic planning team were shared with the larger group. The larger group used the findings as a basis to have conversations to imagine the future of Haverwood Healthcare five years from now. They summarized their conversations as follows:

Strengths: *Exceptional care, long-term resident loyalty, and a culture of daily appreciation for each other including the staff and residents.*

Opportunities: *Provide superior flexible dining service and a daily activity program that engages residents, family members, and local community members.*

Aspirations: *Be the first choice as local provider as a result of the highly qualified, trained and caring staff that creates radiance and energy in the residents' lives.*

Results: *Increase census by 10% within 30 days and train the entire staff on the importance of census development and their role in contributing to this goal.*

The core team also created a tagline that was adopted by the rest of the employees at the facility: *Caring people, Caring for people, in a most Caring place!*

Innovate: *What can we create to achieve our aspirations?*

This phase included a series of meetings with a variety of groups having expertise and interest to help identify specific strategic initiatives needed to strengthen and achieve the opportunities and aspirations and leverage core strengths identified during the Inquiry and Imagine phase. For instance, in an effort to realize the opportunity of superior flexible dining service at Haverwood, the following activities took place:

- A resident council was created to allow residents direct input into meal selection and dining times.
- Outside vendors were brought in and training programs were conducted to improve meal quality.
- Monthly in-services were instituted for all dietary staff.
- A café service was set up to allow residents and family members access to snacks during off hours.
- Restaurant style meals were incorporated, including a menu ordering process.

Each of these activities required the creation of new processes or project plans and a point of contact so someone would be held accountable. Those decisions were made in the Implement phase.

Implement: *How do we move forward to achieve our goals?*
Each new initiative created in the Innovate phase was assigned co-champions in the Implement phase to be responsible to make sure initiatives are *implemented*. The team developed measurable goals, six-month benchmarks, and short-term action steps to know what to do to achieve goals and progress towards benchmarks, and identification of critical stakeholders needed to support the initiative. For example, in order to implement the "superior dining services" initiative, the chef and the dining manager took the lead, and they included those stakeholders that were part of the dining experiences, from the staff and food suppliers to the residents and their family members. In addition, each team was required to measure success and report back to the team. The measures were based upon defined criteria, such as, dining experience, food quality, customer satisfaction, or census growth.

This feedback was used to assess whether the progress was sufficient to achieve the initiative or if further steps were needed. The staff recognized that successful implementation was highly dependent on maintaining the relationship connections made during the Inquire, Imagine, and Innovate phases, and build on the energy and participation of all stakeholders. The progress of the strategic initiatives was communicated to all of the interested stakeholders in an effort to keep them informed, inspired, and engaged. Within six weeks, there were five significant results.

1. The center experienced a 12% increase in new residents.
2. Monthly in-service training was reinstated for all staff on all shifts.
3. The assisted living center became a community gathering place where young members from the community interacted with the seniors.
4. Various departments developed a new spirit of cooperation in serving the residents.
5. Dining hall satisfaction increased from 52% to 89%.

The administrator of the facility stated, "We have seen a dramatic shift from a defensive posture of fear from our employees to a new level of excitement about our ability to truly make the facility into what we want it to be while considering each and every stakeholder."

A Positive Divestiture

After one year, the SOAR strategic plan showed positive results, and the center was a success. However, the story does not end here. Eighteen months later, the state reduced its reimbursement for this type of healthcare facility, making it no longer viable to operate the center. The company made the decision, for the first time in its history, to take the bold step of closing one of its centers due to this significant uncontrollable change in its external environment.

In its 15-year history, Haverwood Healthcare had never closed a facility. This story is different from many strategic planning stories, because instead of resulting in a happy ending or creating amazing long-term financial returns, it resulted in a positive divestiture. It illustrates that strategic planning does not always end in finding new ways to grow a company. However, as a result of using this approach, Haverwood was more resilient and better able to handle the reality of closing down a center.

Closing an assisted living center, which residents consider their home, is not a simple task. Because the staff, residents, families, and management had the opportunity to work together collaboratively to create a strategy and keep the facility open for the previous 18 months, they took this as an opportunity to plan a strategy and smooth transition to close it down. From the date the closure was announced, until the last resident moved out, took less than 30 days. Several noteworthy points include the following:

- During the entire transition, every staff member showed up for work.
- No one left his or her position prematurely.
- The company worked to find employment opportunities for every employee who desired it.
- Every resident was placed without incident into another center.

The State Ombudsman who worked with the center during the closure remarked, "The closure was a model of cooperation, participation, and efficiency."

Because of this successful divestiture, Haverwood went on to use the SOAR framework at its regional and corporate level. In the words of Haverwood Healthcare's Vice President of Business Development, "There is no doubt that the divestiture went as well as it did as a direct result of the work we had done previously using SOAR. The SOAR framework created a dialogue among the stakeholders and received positive buy-in from all stakeholders. We weren't just managers and staff doing a job. We were a community of people working collaboratively to do what was best for our residents and their families. What SOAR offers is a positive approach to the way we think, plan, and act together. It provided us an effective and flexible framework that fosters the energy, creativity, and engagement of all our employees and residents. The results for us were resiliency and a positive environment in such a difficult time."

Using the SOAR framework within the 5-I Cycle enables people to come together to put a strategy or strategic plan in place in an environment where all possible relevant voices are heard. In the next chapter, we provide additional snapshots of case studies to show the flexibility and scalability of SOAR applications.

Key Point of this Chapter

- This chapter provided a detailed example of a SOAR 5-I Cycle to create a strategic plan for a healthcare facility.

Strategic Questions

- How would you introduce SOAR to your team or organization?
- Who would be part of your core team – the strategic planning team?

Chapter 6 / **SOARING AT MULTIPLE LEVELS**

Every organization's and every life's destiny are a series of defining moments – conversations that shape us, change us, and have a huge impact on our development and strategic choices.

— *David Cooperrider*

SOAR has been shown to be a whole system approach to achieve alignment, engagement, and innovation in strategic planning conversations. We have learned that SOAR is effective not just at the top level of the organization but at any level to help both leaders and stakeholders translate or create strategy, strategic plans, and tactical plans. In this chapter, we will share examples of how SOAR is used at multiple levels (division, department, project, team, and individual) within a Fortune 100 global manufacturer.

SOARing at multiple levels is accomplished in a series of conversations. Many of the SOAR questions provided in Chapter 3 can be adapted to any level in the organization as you lead a SOAR session. For each of the levels, we provide you with a short description, recommended approach, and a table of the session's Input, SOAR questions, and Output. We illustrate each level with a case example from a global large equipment manufacturer we call EarthMid Manufacturing.

SOARing at the Division Level

A division (sometimes referred to as Business Unit) level strategy is similar to an organization's strategy. At the division level, the environment, industry trends, and competition still have to be considered. In addition, the division must align to the organization's strategy and deliver their part to support the goals. We recommend conducting a large group SOAR session that goes beyond the top level of management to include the lower levels of management and representation from frontline supervisors and supporting staff.

Division Level SOAR Session

Inputs	Competitive analysis, resource review, and organization strategic plan.
Strengths	What capabilities do we possess that differentiates our division and supports the organization's strategic plan and goals?
Opportunities	What are the most compelling opportunities for our division?
	How can we best deliver initiatives that are aligned with the organization's values, vision, and mission?
	How do we translate the organization's initiatives into our projects?
Aspirations	How can we make a difference for the organization, our division, our employees, and our customer?
	If our division was a new and separate organization, how would we lead our company?
	Where do our strengths and opportunities intersect with our aspirations, so we can focus on the best use of our limited resources?
Results	What measurable indicators do we want to achieve?
	How often should we meet to discuss our progress?
Output	Strategic decisions made on key initiatives, visual high-level timelines and dashboards, translation of the organization's strategy to the division level, input to division level business plan and performance management system.

Division Level Example

The Tractor Division contributed $6 billion to EarthMid's business portfolio. As a division, it was larger than many manufacturing organizations. A new general manager, Mike, wanted to do something different for the division's strategic planning that would achieve the innovation and growth goals within EarthMid's strategic plan. He decided to try SOAR and engaged an internal facilitator to guide the conversations for the division plan. Their first change to the traditional strategic planning was to expand employee participation. Previously, Mike had only involved his senior leadership team and a few subject matter experts.

SOAR-based conversations were initiated by taking the original small group of 12 senior leaders and inviting 68 middle managers and supervisors from across the Tractor Division. To optimize the effectiveness of small groups, ten teams of eight participants were created with a diverse representation of functions and levels (called max-mixed). Direct reports were not at the same table as their immediate supervisor.

The conversations began with the teams of eight, followed by report outs to everyone in the room to create collective understanding. The Strengths conversation reflected on this question: *What capabilities do we possess that can differentiate our division and support the organization in achieving its goals?* The focus was to identify which capabilities created energy, confidence, and pride for what had been accomplished and could be leveraged to grow the division.

The Opportunities conversation began with information about EarthMid's strategic plan and Tractor's industry trends. From this shared foundation, a wall sized mind-map visualized the opportunities, so the participants could brainstorm emerging possibilities. They added their ideas on the wall using self-sticking notes. The ideas were grouped, ranked, and the top five opportunities selected. This process developed alignment for choosing the possibilities that would most impact EarthMid's growth strategy.

The Aspirations conversation started with creative activities designed to help participants, accustomed to managing, to imagine they were the new owners of 'TractorCo.' Taking on an ownership mindset, they moved beyond assumed boundaries to seeing the whole division as entrepreneurs. This uncovered new paths to achieve desired possibilities. With multiple ideas from this exercise, they prioritized opportunities into several compelling strategic initiatives.

The Results conversation defined the measures needed to assess progress. They used a balanced scorecard[30] approach to track and share key strategic initiatives. Participants returned to their departments with greater understanding and buy-in to the strategy and goals. They were able to translate the strategic initiatives into projects. This ensured their direct reports understood and were engaged in the Tractor Division's strategic plan.

SOARing at the Department Level

A department could be functional (e.g. Marketing, HR, Engineering, Quality) or operational (production of the product or service). A department's strategy must support the organization and the division level strategic plan. It balances resources for ongoing operations and the strategic change initiatives. This means prioritization and a realistic allocation of resources.

Department Level SOAR Session

Inputs	Organization strategy, division strategy, division initiatives/ projects, and resource review.
Strengths	What capabilities do we possess that can help our department and best support our division's and the organization's strategy and goals?
Opportunities	What is our part in delivering the division's and organization's initiatives? What could we do differently to best deliver initiatives to divisions that are aligned with the organization's values, vision, and mission?
Aspirations	How can we make a difference for the organization, our divisions, our employees, and our customers? How can we best support our employees, so they develop and effectively grow?
Results	What measurable indicators do we want and when should they be achieved? How often should we meet to review our progress?
Output	Strategic decisions made on key initiatives, visual high-level timelines and dashboards, translation of the organization's strategy to the division level, input to division level business plan and performance management system.

Department Level Example

The Global Law Services (GLS) department had a significant challenge to achieve the organization goals of growth and speed to market for EarthMid. The department's senior leadership realized they needed a shift in both the department's mindset and how they operated. Often, the department's business partners saw GLS as a place where they would hear *no*. GLS needed to become the place business partners went for help with proactive removal of barriers. This would be a fundamental shift in their thinking, so they knew they had to engage everyone in the department. They chose SOAR for their strategy session.

Coordinated planning was needed to schedule GLS leaders that supported 160 world-wide locations. The question was, "how could they create relationships among law service employees across the world while they provided legal services in a timely manner?" The first step to get there was to arrange for more than 40 participants to gather at headquarters. A few of the participants who couldn't make the trip were included virtually. Since a goal was to create relationships, the max-mixed small group tables considered multi-national and multi-levels. This facilitated working together and gaining a greater understanding of each other. Focusing on their strengths and aspirations helped establish a positive atmosphere and openness to change.

Even so, the initial conversation on strengths was challenging since GLS was seen as a barrier to speed to market. In truth, they often felt their value was in slowing things down. The strengths reflection helped them see other ways they had contributed rather than to just provide focus on worst-case scenarios. It encouraged a shift to engage earlier in the product development process in order to mitigate problems. This would also occur more naturally by creating close relationships with engineering and operations.

The Opportunities conversation provided the foundation for GLS's connection to the organization strategy and world trends across legal services functions. It expanded the sense of possibility and contribution with data on how some legal functions were supporting speed. They decided to engage local law firms to handle contract details. Local law firm partners could be more responsive and culturally sensitive for the EarthMid location. This would free up more time for GLS employees to become business partners within EarthMid.

The Aspirations conversation explored rethinking how to truly operate as a GLS team across the world. For example, the top priority that emerged was a project to reorganize the entire department into global product and service support teams. Additional initiatives and projects were identified and communicated through a GLS Business Plan so every GLS employee could have the document on their desk. The Results conversation determined indicators and metrics that showed how GLS supported the divisions and other departments in speed to market efforts.

SOARing at the Project level

Projects are temporary undertakings that deliver change initiatives identified through strategic planning. An important first step for a project is to create a charter that translates the organization, division, or department initiatives into a project. The charter provides clarity for the why and what of this project (case for action), the timeline, and how this project will be accomplished. The charter specifies the team members including leadership, project leads, subject matter experts, and full or part-time team members. SOAR-based conversations are especially helpful for creating a charter.

Project Level SOAR Session

Inputs	Organization, division or department strategy, initiatives, and project vision, mission, and case for action.
Strengths	Who is on our project team and what strengths do they bring?
	What strengths does our organization, division, or department and sponsor team have for this project work?
Opportunities	What difference will this project make to our organization and our customers?
	What strategic initiative(s) does this project forward? How does it forward the initiative?
	How can we best balance scope, schedule, and resources?
	What is the potential for development for the project members?
Aspirations	Can we go beyond the project vision, mission, and case for action to create something more compelling for the organization, customers, and ourselves?
	How can we effectively bring about change while honoring people/stakeholders involved?
Results	What measurable indicators do we want and when should they be achieved?
	How often should we meet to see and discuss our progress?
	How can we celebrate achieving milestones?
Output	Revised charter, project plan, visual roadmap, and dashboards.

Project Level Example

EarthMid's Electronics Engineering (EE) was assigned a project to develop an accelerated process to support innovation for advanced engineering efforts. Engineering leadership provided an initial high-level charter that included the Project Lead and suggestions for team members. Don, the Project Lead had experienced SOAR in the Tractor Division's strategic planning session. He wanted to apply the approach to further define the project and develop the project team's understanding. Don employed an internal facilitator to guide the project definition session. Don and the project team decided to include the entire advanced EE department in the SOAR session to develop the charter.

The Strengths conversation was conducted at two levels. One level was a reflection on EE's capabilities and their networks to product development and leading-edge electronics suppliers. The next level focused on the strengths to deliver on the project goals. This built energy and confidence that an Advanced Innovation Process (AIP) would keep EarthMid as a leading-edge company.

The Opportunities conversation clarified how an innovation process would help to achieve EarthMid's, Tractor's, and EE's strategy. They also investigated the best global EE practices. Finally, they discussed opportunities for the team members potential roles in the future process.

The Aspirations conversation explored the most desired future for AIP and the roles to support it. Building on the Strengths and Opportunities conversations, the project's vision, mission, and goals were shifted for greater innovation and more risk-taking. The conversations provided a more detailed charter and approach to engage more stakeholders. Don and the project team were confident that the future AIP could produce the speed to market for EarthMid's products on time and with the allocated resources.

Being part of the AIP project definition sessions had electronics engineers vying for the project team's adjunct positions. The EE's leadership was astonished at the greater clarity and challenge of the project charter. Everything was in place to accomplish the project goal.

SOARing at the Team Level

The key to a team delivering desired results is for team members to collaborate effectively with each other. Foundational for team success is determining how team members can best work together to deliver results, something we discovered SOAR does well.

Team Level SOAR Session

Inputs	Organization, division, or department strategy and initiatives, and team charter.
Strengths	Who is on our team, and what professional and personal style strengths do they bring?
	What strengths have our organization, department, and leadership developed to support teamwork?
	What has been our best team working experience? What are some best practices for working agreements?
Opportunities	What differences could this team make to our organization, department, and customers?
	What possibilities exist to create collaboration among team members?
Aspirations	How can we work, learn and enjoy each other so we meet and exceed the expected results?
	How can we create effective working agreements to optimize our individual contributions?
Results	How often should we meet to discuss our progress?
	How can we celebrate achieving success?
Output	Working agreements, visual roadmap, and dashboards.

Team Level Example

As reflected in the department level example, the Global Law Service strategic plan resulted in a new organization structure initiative to better support the global reorganization. In the restructuring, new teams and leaders were assigned. Deb, the new leader of Special Litigation, knew she had to reengineer their legal processes, but first she needed to create a great team. The organization development facilitator worked with Deb to design the SOAR session to create a high-performance team. One outcome would be dynamic working agreements. Pre-work for the session had department members take a Myers-Briggs Type Indication (MBTI)[31] assessment to help understand the group dynamics.

The Strengths conversation explored team members' capabilities and an MBTI group strength analysis. The Opportunities conversation built on the Strengths conversation to understand how to leverage strengths and compensate for any weaknesses. The Aspirations conversation reflected on the best team experiences of working and learning collaboratively. The learnings from Strengths, Opportunities, and Aspirations were used as the basis for new working agreements. The Results conversation provided working agreements as a living document to be used in each team meeting and ongoing operations. The agreements defined what the team members could expect from each other in terms of civility, trust, respect, and accountability. The team now had the relationship foundation to develop the global legal processes and new structures.

SOARing at the Individual level

SOAR-based conversations at the individual level use coaching techniques to facilitate development. We define coaching at this level as a committed listener that supports an individual to gain awareness, determine action, and have accountability to their personal growth. Typical uses at the individual level are coaching for new positions, new projects, career development, personal branding, work-life balance, and other developmental efforts. The coach uses SOAR questions in a series of weekly or biweekly one-on-one conversations.

Individual Level SOAR Session

Inputs	Organization, division, department, project, and team strategies.
Strengths	What are your strengths as they relate to this possibility (e.g., new position, project, career aspiration)? What are you most proud of accomplishing since our last session? How does that translate to a new or developing strength?
Opportunities	What opportunities do you see for yourself or for your department, division, or organization in this situation? What opportunities are there for you this week?
Aspirations	What are you most excited to create for yourself and others? Why? What do you find personally compelling? What generates excitement and energy? Why?
Results	What action/goal are you willing to commit to for our next session? What resources do you need? What milestones or results will indicate your progress? When you achieve this new possibility, what now is possible?
Output	Aligned action from internal motivation and commitment that creates success and a feeling of accomplishment, thriving, and flourishing.

Individual Example

As part of a commitment to individual development and the need for continuous global organizational change, EarthMid invested in creating an internal coaching capability. As a result, over 100 executive coaches were developed. New managers often requested these coaches to help them in their new positions. This was especially true if that position was in another country. When Franz, a German national, was assigned as a quality manager for the Tractor Division in the U.S. Midwest, he anticipated challenges and requested a coach. His coach used SOAR for their conversations.

The Strengths conversation allowed Franz to reflect on his technical capability, previous management experience, global perspective, and language proficiency. Franz also realized he had a deep understanding of the division's and quality function's strengths. He knew how his team should fit in.

When exploring opportunities for himself in his new position, he saw that collaboration could increase the quality of the new series tractor. The aspirations that Franz identified was to first create a high-performance team that could deliver the quality processes needed for the new product program. This meant both working on the team's group dynamics, their global quality connection, and his capability as an expatriate manager. His results would be measured by achieving weekly commitments and meeting the quality milestones for the product program.

Through coaching, Franz became willing to call upon any resources to help him create the relationships with his direct reports and develop his team. Franz extended his coaching support beyond the usual six-weeks new manager coaching. He continued coaching for six months which allowed him to build his confidence, improve his thinking, and embrace positive approaches to development. The Weekly Coaching Process table on the right captures another view of the simple coaching approach using SOAR questions.

SOARing at multiple levels provides greater alignment, engagement, and innovation to achieve the organization's strategic goals from anywhere in the organization. It has also been our experience that pausing to reflect on strengths, opportunities, aspirations, and desired results creates the energy needed to meet the day-to-day, short-term, and long-term challenges of growth and change. In the next chapter, we provide some snapshots of case studies to show the flexibility of SOAR.

Weekly Coaching Process

Connect Questions
What's going on for you?

What (possibility) would you like to create (this week)?

Tell me about this possibility.

SOAR Questions

Strengths What are your strengths as they relate to this possibility?

Opportunities What opportunities do you see in this situation?

Aspirations What do you most aspire to create? What is your vision?

Results What action/ goal are you willing to commit to?
What results will indicate your progress?

Commitment Questions
When you create this new possibility, what now becomes possible?

What action and awareness will you commit to for this week?

What resources do you need?

Who could you connect with to further this effort?

Key Point of this Chapter
- This chapter provided guidance to use SOAR conversations for aligned strategy, strategic engagement, strategic planning, and coaching at multiple levels in an organization.

Strategic Questions
- How might SOAR be applied at any level or multiple levels in your organization?
- How would you design SOAR questions to fit the level at which you are working, context, and culture for a strategy session?
- How does SOAR support strategic alignment?
- How might you use SOAR to mentor or coach others to positively impact their performance?

Chapter 7 / **AN INVITATION TO SOAR**

All dreams come true if we have the courage to pursue them.

— *Walt Disney*

We are often asked, who has used SOAR and with what results and learnings. The answer is a wide variety of organizations around the world at the organization, business unit and operating unit levels. SOAR is flexible and scalable; you can use it anywhere in your organization and design an approach to fit your needs and culture. Examples from for-profit, non-profit, and government sectors have been provided throughout this book. In this last chapter, new snapshots are provided.[32] Our goal is two-fold: first is to give you a sense of the many types of organizations, situations, and approaches where SOAR has been successful, and second is to increase your confidence to try SOAR.

1. A global environmental company wants to be the voice of industry and innovation

Organization	A global environmental company
Situation	A broad representation of stakeholders conducted a strategic planning session to imagine how this company can be the "voice of the industry" and share the "purpose of the company" with the world.
Approach	SOAR was integrated with a two-day Appreciative Inquiry Planning Summit with 80 participants across the division, including 15 external stakeholders.
Outcome and Lessons Learned	The SOAR session created a bold shared vision and led to the rapid development of six priority initiatives. One initiative resulted in a cure for the Zika Virus at the local level. The prototype for the cure was created at the summit. This successful outcome resulted in testifying before Congress on how to control Zika based on eradicating the first local transmission in Miami Dade. Another strategic priority created a system to donate 1% of revenues (not profits) to global environmental organizations to "do well by doing good" strategy.

2. A social media organization created innovative solutions of well-being

Organization	A division of R&D in a global social media company
Situation	Internal researchers and a product development team invited external experts in positive psychology to identify innovations to promote the well-being of its user community.
Approach	SOAR and Appreciative Inquiry were used in a two-day strategic design collaboration with 30 internal and external stakeholders.
Outcome and Lessons Learned	SOAR helped overcome the skepticism as to how open the organization was to outside collaboration. Exceeding expectations, the new features identified at the event were implemented across the platform's global user base within five months.

3. A law firm needs to respond effectively to unexpected changes

Organization	A specialty law firm in a large urban area
Situation	State law changes directly impacted the value of law firm's futur cases and fees. In addition, one of the founding partners was kille in an accident. A holistic understanding of the services, clients and roles was needed to respond to the changes and commit t developing for sustainability and growth.
Approach	The firm used SOAR in a 1½ day strategic planning session tha included all attorneys, paralegals, assistants, and staff. The partne and the consultant used pre-work and periodic follow-ups.
Outcome and Lessons Learned	The firm achieved a collective understanding of the impacts of th new laws and the role changes needed to respond to the loss c a founding partner. The team identified and gained appreciatio for the different strengths and contributions of every role. The achieved a whole new level of collaboration. As a result, the fir generated a 33% increase in fees and a 50% increase in profits. Th occurred while competitor firms remained even or lost in the ne legal climate.

4. A new division needed an aligned strategic plan

Organization	Automotive supplier technology division
Situation	The division needed to create a plan to work with automoti related original equipment manufacturers to drive business ar provide revenue growth for the corporation. The division w operating in silos with no shared vision or strategy for growth.
Approach	SOAR and 5-I Cycle guided the strategic planning process.
Outcome and Lessons Learned	New product, service, and market opportunities were identifi based on distinctive capabilities. They created a strategic pl that aligned with the corporation and removed the silos amo the three areas in the division. The session created a profitable a collaborative work environment within the Technology Divisi and corporate headquarters. SOAR was later introduced at corporate level.

5. An organization wanted a positive and successful merger

Organization	A recently merged metropolitan and suburban library system
Situation	The library system was coming out of a merger that had been challenging. They needed to develop a comprehensive and high engagement strategic plan that would guide the organization and its members for the next three years.
Approach	A Quick SOAR was used to design an Appreciative Inquiry (AI) Summit that would involve over 100 participants from various member libraries.
Outcome and Lessons Learned	Six strategic initiatives and 20 goals were identified for the next three years. The board members and employees became highly engaged in the process. Innovation and healing came from hearing diverse stakeholder voices. Members of the library system are utilizing SOAR for their strategic planning efforts.

6. A strategic integration of international sales teams in a global hospitality merger

Organization	An international hotel chain
Situation	When two major hotel organizations merged, the sales teams needed an integrated sales strategy to support the new global hotel chain.
Approach	SOAR and 5-I Cycle were used to engage the sales teams in a dialogue to create a strategic plan for the regional sales division. SOAR was used for strategic exploration, visioning, action planning, and creating a communication strategy.
Outcome and Lessons Learned	SOAR engaged the team in dialogue on expectations, methods of communication, alignment of sales teams' mission, strategies, and goals. There was an effective integration of the two separate organization's sales teams into one that supports the new organization.

7. An annual personal development event

Organization	Business and life coaching organization
Situation	This organization had a large community of members from over 75 countries. They held a three-day, highly immersive event that helped 450+ attendees design personal development plans for the next one to three years.
Approach	A facilitator used the SOAR framework to lead attendees through the design of personal plans to become the best version of themselves. Attendees were taken through exercises to discover their strength and highest purpose. Each designed specific strategies and action plans to move towards their highest aspirations over the next six to 24 months.
Outcome and Lessons Learned	Starting with a deep connection to personal strengths and compelling visions for what matters most led to significant improvement in attendee energy. Attendees wrote specific plans to achieve the results. Many attendees chose to join accountability groups with others to build on the momentum. The event and community have grown as the result of the attendee experience guided by SOAR.

8. An organization dedicated to those facing life-threatening illnesses + their families

Organization	A non-profit organization
Situation	Stakeholders including the board of directors, past recipients, donors, and families come together annually to plan the future of the organization and create a positive impact for attendees and their families.
Approach	SOAR was integrated into a two-day Appreciative Inquiry strategic planning event with 80 attendees, including 40 kids (under the age of 12).
Outcome and Lessons Learned	SOAR gave individuals the opportunity to connect with personal strengths, opportunities, aspirations, and action plans. The non-profit broadly expanded the stakeholders and perspectives represented. Inviting the participants to design solutions for the future of the organization increased buy-in, enthusiasm for, and ultimately execution of high priority opportunities.

9. IT leaders from 17 federal government agencies

Organization	Federal government agencies
Situation	Seventeen federal government agencies came together for the first time to work across agencies to share information and discover how to strengthen the government's IT infrastructure.
Approach	SOAR was used at a three-day offsite to create a collaborative framework of sharing relevant information with 97 IT leaders.
Outcome and Lessons Learned	The outcome was a framework with high-levels plans that incorporated the best ideas from the employees in their respective federal agencies. People had a shared mission and strategy on how to share information, and understood where the data makes a contribution to other agencies.

These snapshots demonstrate that SOAR has many applications at the individual, team, division, and organization level. Strategy or strategic planning is not just an annual review of budgets, goals, and objectives nor is it a quarterly financial ritual. Instead, SOAR is a 21st century strategic thinking, planning, and leading framework that engages the whole system. It is designed for agility and responsiveness. SOAR should be thought of as an approach that provides a flexible framework allowing stakeholders to connect, reconnect, and adjust to real-time innovations and feedback.

By using SOAR's whole system approach to strategic planning, we have been privileged to experience many and varied organizations rekindling their positive core and re-energizing their stakeholders. SOAR sustains the values of an organization while honoring the knowledge, capabilities, and spirit of its members. Helping to bring organizational members' spirit back to their work is an unquantifiable personal benefit.

Every time we have guided a team, division, or an organization or coached colleagues through SOAR, we have been guided as well. SOAR has become part of our DNA. It is hard to imagine any future strategy, action, or plan without considering where it is strong, what the opportunities are, what we really want to happen, and what would indicate progress and success. As problems and challenges are presented, reframing the problem and looking for strengths and opportunities while inquiring into aspirations and desirable results has become automatic. Implementing SOAR should be tailored to the specific situation and culture. In sum, SOAR is flexible and scalable in its application so that anyone can make strategy part of his or her job. We hope you have also been inspired and that you accept the invitation to SOAR!

Key Point of this Chapter
• This chapter provided many examples of using the SOAR framework.

Strategic Questions
• How would you use SOAR to create a strategy that positively impacts your organization, division, department, project, team, or yourself?
• How can you share your experience with us?

Vision is manifested in values and action.

Mission is defined by values and vision.

Goals are created based on mission.

Strategies are how to achieve goals.

Objectives are actions to support strategies.

Strategic initiatives support objectives.

A plan details strategic initiatives.

Actions move forward from a plan.

Change requires choices and action!

— *Jacqueline M. Stavros*

1. Stavros, J.M. (2013). The Generative Nature of SOAR: Applications, Results, and the new SOAR Profile, *Appreciative Inquiry Practitioner*, Volume 15, Number 3, ISBN: 978 1-907549-16-8, www.aipractitioner.com.

2. Stavros J.M., & Torres, C. (2018). *Conversations Worth Having: Using Appreciative Inquiry to Fuel Productive and Meaningful Engagement*, Oakland, CA: Berrett-Koehler Publishers.

3. SOAR questions are generative questions with two qualities: 1: they change how people think so new options for decisions and actions become available and 2: they stimulate compelling images people act on. For more information see: Bushe, G. (2013). Generative Process, Generative Outcomes: The Transformation Potential of Appreciative Inquiry. In D.L. Cooperrider et al., eds., *Organizational Generativity: The Appreciative Inquiry Summit and a Scholarship of Transformation, Volume 4, Advances in Appreciative Inquiry*, Bingley, UK: Emerald Publishers, 89-113.

4. Cooperrider, D. (2018). Introduction: We Live in Worlds Our Conversations Create. In J.M. Stavros & C. Torres, *Conversations Worth Having: Using Appreciative Inquiry to Fuel Productive and Meaningful Engagement* (p. 3), Oakland, CA: Berrett-Koehler Publishers.

5. In his video, *Celebrate What's Right with the World*, Dewitt Jones advocates using a positive mindset to deal with change. He also says, "Connect with a vision that opens us to possibilities and gives us the courage to soar." For more information visit http://www.dewittjones.com or https:// starthrower.com/.

6. Also, a life-giving force can be represented in a single moment, such as a particular customer engagement service that went above and beyond expectations.

7. For more information on Appreciative Inquiry (AI), please visit the AI Commons at https://appreciativeinquiry.champlain.edu/. The AI Commons offers resources and practical tools on AI and the rapidly growing discipline of strengths-based positive change.

8. Newest definition of Appreciative Inquiry socially constructed in a conversation by David L. Cooperrider, Lindsey Godwin, and Jackie Stavros (personal communication: August 12, 2018).

9. For a quick Introduction to Appreciative Inquiry (AI), please see the *Thin Book of Appreciative Inquiry* by Sue Annis Hammond (2013) in its third edition which has more how-to tips to get started.

10. To read more on how to transform your organization differently than 10 routine change programs refer to Isern, J., & Pung, C. (2007). Driving Radical Change. The *McKinsey Quarterly*, #4, pp. 1-12. McKinsey has a lot of helpful research on strategy and leading change at https:// www.mckinsey.com/quarterly/overview.

11. Laszlo, C., & Zhexembayeva, N. (2011). *Embedded Sustainability: The Next Big Competitive Advantage*, Stanford, CA: Stanford Business Books.

12. To learn more, we have a list of strategy books that we recommend on page 66.

13. Rath T., & Conchie, B. (2009). *Strengths-Based Leadership*, New York: Gallup Press or visit https:// www.gallupstrengthscenter.com.

14. Daly, A., Millhollen, B., & DiGuilio, L., (2007). SOARing Toward Excellence in an Age of Accountability: The Case of the Esperanza School District. *AI Practitioner*. www.aipractitioner.com.

15. Cameron, K. (2013). *Practicing Positive Leadership*, pp.2-3, Oakland, CA: Berrett-Koehler Publishers.

16. Fredrickson, B. (2009). *Positivity: Groundbreaking Research Reveals How to Embrace the Hidden Strength of Positive Emotions, Overcome Negativity, and Thrive.* New York: Crown Publishers.

17. Losada, M., & Heaphy, E. (2004). The role of positivity and connectivity in the performance of business teams: A nonlinear dynamics model. *American Behavioral Scientist*, 47(6), 740 765. http://dx.doi.org/10.1177/0002764203260208.

18. Cameron, K. (2012). *Positive Leadership: Strategic for Extraordinary Performance,* Oakland, CA: Berrett- Koehler Publishers.

19. Cameron, K., & Lavine, M. (2006). *Making the Impossible Possible: Leading Extraordinary Performance: The Rocky Flats Story,* Oakland, CA: Berrett-Koehler Publishers.

20. The search for positive meaning has been proposed as a universal human need in the works of Baumesiter & Vohs (2002), Frankl (1959), and Grant (2007) as cited in K. Cameron (2012). *Positive Leadership: Strategies for Extraordinary Performance*, (pp.67-68), Oakland, CA: Berrett-Koehler Publishers.

21. Isern, J., & Pung, C. (2007). Driving Radical Change. *The McKinsey Quarterly*, N4, p. 3.

22. This question is from the classic book by *Collins, J. (2001). Good to Great: Why Some Companies Make the Leap ... and Others Don't,* New York: Harper Collins Publishers, Inc.

23. For more information on how to engage whole systems and large systems see Change It Up app at www.NEXUS4change.com.

24. To learn more about NECC's senior leadership team's decision to use SOAR and how they used SOAR, watch: https://www.youtube.com/watch?v=NQNTyGLsnCY and how NECC embedded SOAR and AI into its culture: https://www.necc.mass.edu/discover/institutional initiatives/appreciative-inquiry/.

25. President Lane Glenn's one-minute open invitation to SOAR: https://www.youtube.com/watch? v=qr8T7E_niJc and the invitation to SOAR and results achieved, Voices 2012-2015: https:// www.youtube.com/watch?v=H_FglqEQ0U0.

26. Story reprinted with permission from *Appreciative Inquiry Practitioner*, Featured Choice by Stavros, J. (2013). The Generative Nature of SOAR: Applications, Results, and the New SOAR Profile, V15, N3, pp. 7-30, ISBN: 978-1-907549-16-8 (www.aipractitioner.com).

27. The choice to use an internal or external facilitator depends on if all members want to participate in the strategic planning event.

28. To learn more about mind-mapping see https://www.mindmapping.com/.

29. Generative questions are questions you do not have the answer to. It allows you to have a conversation with others that adopt an attitude of curiosity. When

dealing with any issue, generative questions make unseen information visible, stories are shared, feelings are heard, and result in conversations that create trust, positive energy, a positive core, and a pathway forward. To learn more about AI practice of generative questions, see Stavros, J. & Torres, C. (2018). *Conversations Worth Having: Using Appreciative Inquiry to Fuel Productive and Meaningful Engagement*, (pp 54-62), Oakland, CA: Berrett-Koehler Publishers.

30. Balanced Scorecard is a strategic management system use to align the everyone's work with strategy and help to measure internal and external outcomes of the organization. To learn more go to: https://www.balancedscorecard.org/BSC-Basics/About-the-Balanced-Scorecard.

31. For more information on MBTI see: https://www.myersbriggs.org/my-mbti personality-type/mbti-basics/. There are many group dynamic assessments that could be utilized. Selection should fit the organization culture.

32. Thank you to Jon Berghoff and Scot Lowry from the Flourishing Leadership Institute (FLI) that provided SOAR snapshots 1, 2, 7 and 8. Learn more about FLI at https://www.lead2flourish com/.

RECOMMENDED BOOKS ON STRATEGY

deKluyver, C., & Pearce, J. (2011). *Strategy a View from the Top* (4th Edition). Pearson.

Kim, C., & Mauborgne, R. (2015). *Blue Ocean Strategy, Expanded Edition: How to Create Uncontested Market Space and Make the Competition Irrelevant.* Harvard Business School Press.

McKeown, M. (2016). *The Strategy Book: How to Think and Act Strategically to Deliver Outstanding Results* (2nd Edition). FT Press.

Montgomery, C. (2012). *The Strategist: Be the Leader Your Business Needs.* Harper Business.

Rumelt, R. (2017). *Good Strategy/Bad Strategy: The Difference and Why It Matters.* Profile Books.

Thompson, A., Peteraf, M., Gamble, J., & Strickland, A. (2017). *Crafting and Executing Strategy: Concepts* (21st Edition). McGraw-Hill Education.

Acknowledgments

No book is the product of authors alone, and this one is no different. Creating a book takes a great deal of time, effort, and depth of conversations with many people.

We are tremendously grateful and want to especially thank those who have helped to shape SOAR: Major Loyd Beal, III, Jon Berghoff, Matt Cole, David Cooperrider, Lindsey Godwin, Tom Griffin, Jill Hinrichs, Jennifer Hitchcock, Lynn Kelley, Lori Kuehn, Scot Lowry, Deborah Maher, Richard Marburger, Mo McKenna, Pat Pinkston, Cheryl Richardson, Dan Saint, Tony Silbert, Marge Schiller, Ally Stavros, and Cheri Torres. Thank you to the devoted SOAR practitioners and researchers whose ideas, applications, and editorial advice strengthen this book.

We acknowledge the helpful insights and feedback from the students at Lawrence Technological University's College of Business and Information Technology who provided thoughtful critiques and applications of SOAR.

We want to express sincerest appreciation and gratitude Sue Hammond, our first publisher and editor, who had the creative idea of bringing SOAR to life in her Thin Book Series (www.thinbook.com) by publishing two editions of *The Thin Book of SOAR*. Thank you for your unconditional support and guidance as we transition it to *Learning to SOAR*.

Specials thanks to our husbands, Paul Stavros and John Hinrichs, who both provided critical reviews. And, we thank both our Adams, plus our families and friends for their support and patience during the long writing and editing hours.

We are grateful to all of you!

— *Jackie and Gina*

About the Authors

JACQUELINE (JACKIE) STAVROS, DM

Jackie is Professor at Lawrence Technological University's College of Business and IT. She works with organizations in leadership development, team-building, and strategic planning. She is recognized for her creation of SOAR (www.soar-strategy.com). She works with organizations in leadership development, team-building, and strategic planning. She has worked across all sectors: for-profit, non-profit, government, and a wide spectrum of industries. She has presented her research and work in over 25 countries using AI and SOAR to enrich the lives of thousands of people and improve their organizations capacity to thrive and flourish. She has co-authored books, book chapters, and articles in AI, SOAR, and organization development. Her latest book is *Conversations Worth Having: Using Appreciative Inquiry to Fuel Productive and Meaningful Engagement.*

CONTACT: jstavros@ltu.edu

GINA HINRICHS, PH.D.

Gina has consulted for more than twenty years with a range of organizations from companies with $20 billion in sales to education and social profit organizations. Currently, she works as a CARA consultant as an Organization Change Management (OCM) Project Lead.

Gina has written, co-authored and edited several book chapters and articles. She has a BA, BS, MBA, MOB, and a PhD in Organization Development. Gina is an adjunct professor of Strategy and Organization Development courses for several universities.

CONTACT: ghinrichs517@gmail.com

To learn more about SOAR, visit: www.soar-strategy.com

"This book is a must read for everyone engaged in strategic change. SOAR framework is brilliant! I have experienced exceptional results applying SOAR principles in the government. SOAR is easy to use and offers a holistic, strengths-based and positive approach to strategic decision-making necessary for enterprise transformation. From small to large and even complex organizations such as the U.S. Department of Defense have benefited from SOAR."

– Colonel Loyd Beal, III, Acquisition Officer, United States Army

"The National Health Services and Mental Health Services in the United Kingdom benefit so much from incorporating SOAR into our work. The SOAR questions provided enhance my practice and strengthen our mental health recovery work with service users and care givers. I see the energy and commitment to action in the room gather when we work through strengths, opportunities, aspirations, and results. I am pleased to see so much knowledge condensed into this book and the practical examples make strategy part of everyone's job in the real world of work. Thank you, Jackie and Gina for a nugget of gold and pearls of wisdom!"

– Dr. Lyn Williams, Head of Mental Health Services,
National Health Services

"Engagement and Innovation are critical for our organization to be successful in the future. SOAR is a flexible framework we can employ at all levels to gain the alignment to our vision and achieve the engagement and innovation we need. This book is a simple and practical guide to get going on achieving a positive vision."

– Brian Hampton, Enterprise Business Readiness Lead, Walgreens Co.

Made in the USA
Columbia, SC
18 February 2023

12424371R00039